The cooperation and
assistance of members of the
Harvard University community
in the preparation of this
book is greatly appreciated.

Photographs © 1982 by Steve Dunwell
All rights reserved
This book or portions thereof may not be
reproduced in any form without permission
of Foremost Publishers, Inc.
ISBN 0-940078-02-3
Edited by James B. Patrick
Designed by Donald Paulhus
Printed in Japan
Published by Foremost Publishers Inc.
Little Compton, R.I. 02837

HARVARD

A LIVING PORTRAIT

Photography by Steve Dunwell, Introduction by David McCord

Years and years ago, but in my time at Harvard, Sir Donald Tovey, still the ascending critic and musicologist of Edinburgh, lectured to us on Beethoven. Not in the lecture I heard him give, but in his extraordinary, amiable, and often witty prose, he ultimately examined the Ninth Symphony literally stave by stave. So now a fine photographer, Steve Dunwell of Boston, has examined through something like eleven thousand photographs, of which one hundred and twenty-four comprise this book, the visible symphony of our College and University — Harvard and Radcliffe — in depth and in minute detail: brick, stone, doorways, windows, towers, stairwells, rooms, studies; libraries, laboratories; nooks, crannies, trees, shrubs, ivy; the campus which we call the Yard; the strange composite charm of the physical ambiance itself. This is not a book of people, students, faculty, librarians, administrators, scholars, and athletes. It is simply the clear anatomy of academe: a sojourn and a journey all in one.

A sojourn and a journey through pages wholly suited to a triple audience: to Harvard and Radcliffe students, faculty, and staff, past and present; to the thousands of Harvard visitors day in day out who may remember nothing but the half-believable look of the tranquil ancient Yard and the unbelievable reality of the precious Glass Flowers in the Museum of Comparative Zoölogy; and to those who have actually never set foot in Cambridge, but have often wondered: "Who is Sylvia? What is she?" A book, in short, to offer at once a conspectus for those who know or think they know their Harvard; a stunning folio of remembrance for those who seek the *déjà vu;* and a revelation to those who have not yet passed through the gate over which it says with confidence undiminished after all these years: *Enter to Grow in Wisdom.*

As of course, if that directive were actually followed by an undergraduate or graduate student, the growing would naturally advance season by season; so with this book in your hand, for the photographs are arranged by seasons. And arranged with a sensitive control of continuity. Now no sequence of pictures of anything, architecture and environment included, can be expected to flow as with the exquisite primitive mitering of those lofty stones in Machu Picchu, or with the classical guitar in Francisco Tárrega's lovely "Caprichio Arabe"; but all the same, this book is not without a bit of magic in the inevitability of its visual progress page to page and season to season.

Now when young Francis Parkman wrote *The Oregon Trail* in 1846, he had crossed the wide Missouri into a frontier history of which he is himself a part. Henry David Thoreau, six years Parkman's senior, did his travelling round and on a Concord pond named Walden; and for him as for Parkman — as indeed for Emerson in Emerson's own words — "art is the path of the creator to his work." And just as it was with those two sons of Harvard, so it was with the ethic of their College; and so it is philosophically with their University today. Had Parkman and Thoreau been equipped with the fool-proof cameras and color film of the 1980s, what a pictorial record would be ours of a time now totally vanished! As Whitman, another but non-Harvard contemporary, two years Thoreau's junior, has said: "All music is what wakes you when you are reminded by the instruments."

Well, the instruments in this book, being in fact such shrewd but random impressions of what was seen in varying light and often shot from surprising angles, have assembled themselves to waken or remind you, page after page, in the exact measure of the ranging intelligence you would bring, let us say, to the galleries of a great museum. Indeed, come to think of it, you will be — you already *are* — inside a museum.

Consider first the Harvard Yard. Much as L'Enfant laid out the city of Washington, the ghost of Euclid may have had a hand in arranging — reading clockwise — the old north part of the Yard with the bricks of Massachusetts and Harvard Halls, Hollis, little Holden Chapel, Stoughton, Holworthy, tremendous Thayer, and Bulfinch's University Hall made of granite. Why, so compact, so orderly, so tidy is this area that the lenses of two eyes are wide-angled enough to take it all in at a glance.

Harvard has had many architects. The names of some that I forget will occur to you as you study the photographs. I think offhand of Bulfinch, Richardson, Coolidge, Shepley, Le Corbusier, Ware & Van Brunt (Memorial Hall), Gropius, Sert, Stanford White, Stubbins; and Yamasaki. Now it is certain that not every reader will find a picture of everything he or she is looking for; but how can this be helped? I myself miss, for example, a closeup view of any one of the splendid medallions — say a particular starfish — on the glass and bronze doors of the Biology Laboratory: the work (and a masterpiece to my mind) of the sculptor Katharine Lane Weems. Other readers, however, will be surprised and delighted by something here and there never noticed until now. In my forty-six years at Harvard there must have been a dozen doorways in all that thrombus of structures which I never entered. But for the average alumnus or alumna, and for all who *really* know their Harvard and Radcliffe, what this book almost promises is to bring back instantly and vividly some bright fragment of an event half forgotten. I well remember coming out of Jefferson Laboratory from a physics class (electrons and radium) and looking up into an empty blue sky in the nick of time to see a meteor (asteroid) explode by day,

But soundless with the stale report
Of ancient wars and dragon snort.

What a sight! And I also remember — reminded even as I sampled the early drafts of this book — stepping out of the Faculty Club one late autumn night to find myself for one rare, rare, impossible moment standing precisely beneath the open cone of a brilliant aurora borealis display, and looking up into that awesome distance through the grandure hanging above me as if into a godlike, frightening infinity.

Returning to that physics laboratory and to physics: everything in the pages which follow reminds me of my 1921 classmate and fellow concentrator in that abstruse field. He was Leopold D. Mannes, nephew of Walter Damrosch, himself a fine musician who as a freshman was, surprisingly enough, the holder of a number of international patents in color photography. Together he and I built a telescope and with it looked on the available moons of Jupiter and (I think) on the faint rings of Saturn. But his great accomplishment with his co-inventor, Leopold Godowsky, was to do the research which led to Kodachrome and the Franklin medal. Something of Leo is therefore in these words of mine in a book which his genius helped make possible.

As for Radcliffe College, now an integral part of Harvard, in 1979 I said, in a rarely-used verse form called "runover rhyme", what seemed to me important to say on the occasion of her one hundreth anniversary. I thought at the time — and I still think — that runover rhyme suited the nature of this celebration better than the sestina, or English-Greek sapphics, two forms which I rejected.

Radcliffe in Runover Rhyme

Radcliffe, you never could cherish
it. Perish the thought of a C!
Your primitive sundial and gnomon
in Roman employ X, I, V—
alone, or combining these three.

Yet now, as you reach your centennial,
many'll tell you: Don't break
with tradition! But C, as you earn it,
is—durn it—just what you must take:
C, hundred; C, candle; C, cake.

No talk of us being your betters.
All letters are yours to invoke:
A, Agassiz; B, Briggs; C, Comstock—
where *I'm* stuck, for rhyming's no joke.
Bless your alphabet's English as spoke

in those Jamesian days: Neilson, Baker
(caretaker of theater); Doc
and the Choral Society, glorious
Praetorius . . . Horner and Bok,
present Presidents, such was pre-Rock.

In the gym toiled a ballet in bloomers.
Rumors of wars hot or cold
hadn't reached you, dear Lady-in-Waiting
creating—too young to grow old.
Lady Mowlson, Ann Radcliffe: behold

all these pleiads of scholars, of teachers;
outreachers in science, in art;
astronomers, doctors, achievers;
believers in something apart
in the head undivorced from the heart;

revelation that made Helen Keller
your stellar alumna, revered
to this day. Is her Greek *analeptic*
(not *septic*) a word unendeared?
By your light, up through darkness she steered.

So it be. Let us say life was given,
not driven. These hundred years on,
"The habitual vision . . ." before us,
to chorus: The Queen, not the pawn!
It is day. What you've had was the dawn.

If you will accept that notion of looking at this book as though you were in the gallery of some great museum, consider what it is to face a landscape by Corot, Peter De Windt, Bierstadt, or Innes, unable to name the trees, valleys, flowers, rivers, mountains, and then (as by magic) to be given all these variants in detail, and out of them reassemble the painting or watercolor itself. Take such a view, and this book should help you to answer Shakespeare's question: "Who is Sylvia? What is she?" But all I can do to assist the reader who has *never* seen Harvard is to quote myself in the following summary of what my College and my University have meant — and mean — to me:

Harvard has given great men and great ideas and great citizens and great teachers to the nation; she has seen us through nearly a dozen wars. She has given us six presidents of our country; she has stood like a rock in our midst. She has weathered criticism just and unjust, and abuse which is never just; she has looked at her own faults, which have been not a few, and has striven to correct them. She is far from perfect, but she knows that perfection is nothing more than the perpetual will to seek it. If she was ever the rich man's college, she is just as much the poor man's college today; for her sole requirement of the entering student is that he or she have character, ambition, ability, and the capacity to learn to think for himself — for herself. She is not prejudiced with respect to race or creed or color. She is able and eager to help those who enter her gates. She is anxious to be one thing above all: a better Harvard tomorrow than she was yesterday. To that end, she is permanently for change, but always with an eye to the unchanging values of the human spirit. Lastly, and most important, she has faithfully stood for freedom of the mind and the dignity of the individual; and never more so than in the strange, abrasive period which has followed World War II. As one alumnus once wrote to my office: This gift is "for the institution that represents one of the great achievements of American democracy."

David McCord

Overleaf: Lowell House and beyond to the Charles River

An entrance to Kirkland House

Blossoming at Peabody Terrace

Sunrise silhouettes Adams, Lowell towers

Vibrant dogwood at Austin Hall

Late afternoon on the Quadrangle

Griffin and ivy with summertime student, Robinson Hall

Ivied clock at Westmorely Court, Adams House   *Overleaf:* Bridging a lavender Charles

Dusk at Widener Library

Harry Elkins Widener portrait hangs over entablatured fireplace in Memorial Room of his library.

Twin chimneys at Harvard Hall

Faculty Room, University Hall

Recumbent cramming at Quincy House Library

Fresh air tutorial, Aiken Computation Laboratory   *Overleaf:* Knifing the Charles past Mellon Hall

From Eliot Tower, a circular vantage of Kirkland House

Memorial to Harvard's fallen knights of World War I

Track officials confer at Dillon Bowl

The kick – 1000 meter race at Harvard Stadium

Harvard Advocate covers on display

Afternoon at University Hall

Precious Tibetan Buddhist manuscripts, Yenching Library

Solitary study in sun-splashed Eliot House Library

Radcliffe crew, from Weeks Bridge

Tandem stroking past Leverett Towers and Dunster House *Overleaf:* Amiable company in the Harvard Yard

Scowling stone fountain at Adams House

Bicycles and bridged walkway at Westmorely Court North, Adams House

Trenchant thought, preserved at Houghton Library

Thesis struggle under towering tomes at Dunster House

Topographic planning for Jerusalem, Gund Hall

Studying Roman Sculpture, Fogg Museum

Maillol's "Ile de France," Fogg Museum   *Overleaf:* Autumn ivy engulfs lintel on Emerson Hall

Autumn rain, Harvard Yard

From the Class of 1880, the classical gateway beside Lamont Library

Meditation in Memorial Church

Memorial Church celebrates fall

Sunlit exam at Memorial Hall

Dunster House arabesque

Modern dance, Freshman Union

The wooden galleries of Sanders Theater   *Overleaf:* Pre-game warm-up, Harvard Stadium

Harvard writ large

Tailgate repast before Harvard-Yale confrontation

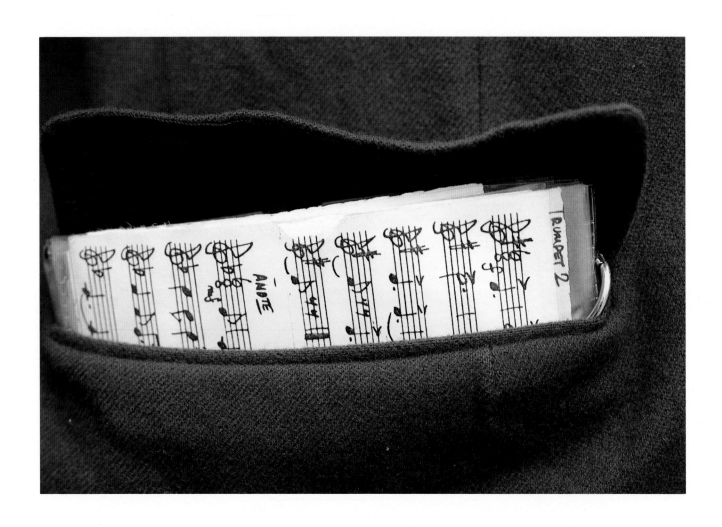

Victory music

Piccolo player, Harvard Band

Gateway to Soldiers Field

Muddy gladiator   *Overleaf:* Crimson ivy festoons Memorial Hall

Heraldic and leafy designs at Lowell House

Sure-footed perch at the Signet Society

John Harvard, by Daniel Chester French

A tour of the Yard

A Hasty Pudding performance begins

Radial translucency at the Science Center

Ivy and Veritas, 17 Quincy Street

Christmas at Kirkland House

Medieval sheet music, Houghton Library

Chorus rehearses Brahms' *Requiem* at Sanders Theater

Elizabethan dancers celebrate Christmas, Fogg Museum   *Overleaf:* News center at The Science Center

Research at Widener Library

Grand staircase, Widener Library

Finals, Memorial Hall

Moment of truth, Memorial Hall

Racing the exam clock at Memorial Hall

Umbrella'd dash at Widener Library

Black tie opening at Houghton Library

Wrestlers take ten, Indoor Athletic Building

Radcliffe takes the ice at Bright Hockey Center

The Yard – Hollis, Stoughton and Holworthy Halls

Plympton Street gateway to Adams House

Fresh snow at the Business School

Unscheduled respite at Dunster Street   *Overleaf:* Winter – and the colonnade at Widener Library

Convergence near Matthews Hall

Serried group photos, spectators, and a lunge – Indoor Athletic Building

John Harvard, unmoved by professional dialogue

Into the warmth of Carpenter Center

Snow shrouds Memorial Church

The dormers of Eliot House

Memorial Church window, and Canady Hall   *Overleaf:* Lunch alfresco in Radcliffe Garden

Willows at Leverett Towers

The cherry trees of Carpenter Center

The Adams House raft race – a noisy acquatic finish at Weld Boat House

Reunion steward at the rail of a Charles River steamer

Tortoise shele from Nanking

University Museum

Kwakiutl house post, Peabody Museum

Skeletal ground sloth, Museum of Comparative Zoology *Overleaf:* Mill Street facade, Lowell House tower

Another drive, another run for Harvard at Soldiers Field

Lacrosse on the Business School Field

A red rose for a well-read student

Collecting Spanish exams, Emerson 101

Concentration – and sharp pencils

Twilit domes of Kirkland and Eliot towers

125

Ceramic ship on a sea of brick at the Lampoon

Under Weeks Bridge at dusk

Overleaf: First in the mind – then, finally, in the hand

Tercentenary Theater; the exhilarating jostle of commencement

Columnar perspective at Widener.

Baccalaureate reception, Busch-Reisinger Museum

Banners high, reunited classes join the commencement parade

Capping in newsprint, Tercentenary Theater

Required reading

Nervous, happy expectancy

Baccalaureate address, Memorial Church

Class of '14.

Mentors in appropriately brilliant enrobement

The "Tree Spread" lunch, Holden Chapel

Strawberries, champagne, conversation at alumni lunch

Faces, and memories, from an earlier time

Spontaneous camaraderie

Exit Eliot House in joy, jubilance, friendship